Combat Sports

WRESTLING

GAIL TERP

BOLT

Bolt is published by Black Rabbit Books
P.O. Box 227, Mankato, Minnesota, 56002.
www.blackrabbitbooks.com

Rhea Magaro, designer;
Alissa Thielges, editor

Library of Congress Cataloging-in-Publication Data
Names: Terp, Gail, 1951- author.
Title: Wrestling / by Gail Terp.
Description: Mankato, MN: Black Rabbit Books, 2025. | Series: Combat sports | Includes bibliographical references and index. | Audience: Ages 8–12 | Audience: Grades 4–6 | Summary: “Get ready for strong holds and quick takedowns in this hi-lo nonfiction chapter book about wrestling. Reluctant readers learn about the skills and training needed to compete on both an amateur and pro level and will be inspired by champions in this combat sport”—Provided by publisher.
Identifiers: LCCN 2024011810 (print) | LCCN 2024011811 (ebook) | ISBN 9781644666876 (library binding) | ISBN 9781644667057 (ebook)
Subjects: LCSH: Wrestling—Juvenile literature.
Classification: LCC GV1195.3 .T47 2025 (print) | LCC GV1195.3 (ebook) | DDC 796.812—dc23/eng/20240318
LC record available at https://lccn.loc.gov/2024011810
LC ebook record available at https://lccn.loc.gov/2024011811

Printed in the United States of America

Image Credits

Alamy Stock Photo/dpa, 4–5, Igor Kralj, 24, Nippon News, 6, ZUMA Press, 12; Associated Press/Hiroto Sekiguchi/Yomiuri Shimbun, 29 (b); Getty Images/4x6, cover, 14–15, 22–23, Anadolu, 28 (t), Andrej Isakovic, 28 (b), Jono Searle, 17 (t), LdF, 26, Pixsell/MB Media, 29 (t), Tim Clayton – Corbis, 19; Shutterstock/Ahturner, 1, 32, ai_stock, 15, AlexandrBognat, 25, Arthur Cauty, 21, Evgeniia Shikhaleeva, 9 (t), FOTOKITA, 3, GTS Productions, 9 (b), Hector Sanchez, 22, Jacob Lund, 10–11, OSTILL is Franck Camhi, 31, Tom Rose, 25; Wikimedia Commons/Alexander Gardner, 17 (b)

Contents

CHAPTER 1

The Bout

Two wrestlers stand ready. The referee blows a whistle and the **bout** begins. The wrestlers grab each other's arms. Each tries to force the other down to the mat and take control. If they do, it's called a **takedown**.

Wrestling strengthens the whole body.

A Winner!

One wrestler grabs her **opponent's** leg. She twists hard. Wham! Her opponent falls. A takedown! But the bout isn't over yet. It lasts two periods. Both wrestlers fight hard. In the end, the first wrestler pins her opponent shoulders to the mat. One second, two seconds. That's all it takes. She wins the bout!

CHAPTER 2

What is Wrestling?

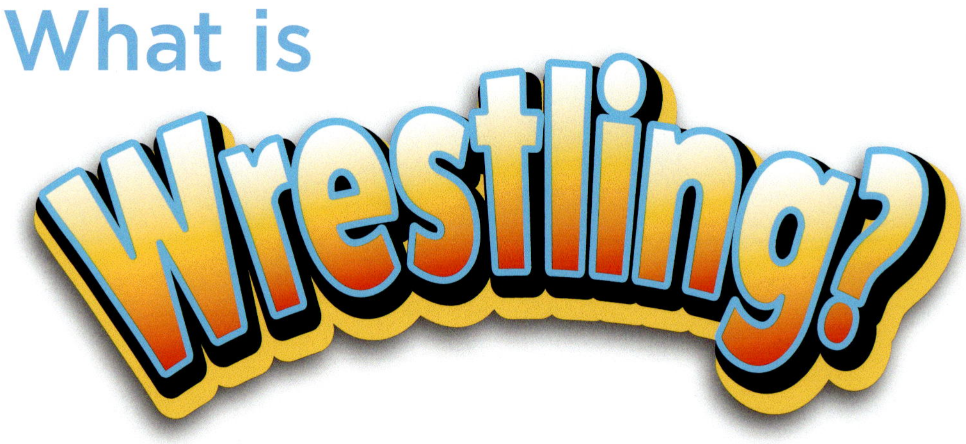

Wrestling is the world's oldest combat sport. The goal is to pin an opponent. Wrestlers do not punch or kick. Instead, they hold onto their opponents. They try to force them to the mat. They can also lift and throw their opponents.

Wrestling Styles

Freestyle Wrestlers

hold above and below waist
use legs to hold

Greco-Roman Wrestlers

only hold above the waist
cannot use legs to hold

Training for Strength

Wrestlers train hard. They need to be strong. Strength gives their moves more power. It gives wrestlers **endurance**. It helps improve balance.

Wrestlers also work on their skills. They practice moves over and over. They want their moves to be **automatic**.

Wrestlers lift weights as part of their training.

Taking Down an Opponent

Takedowns are important moves. They put a wrestler in control. There are several types. In one, a wrestler grabs their opponent's leg and pushes them to the mat. In another, a wrestler slings an opponent onto their shoulders. Then they throw the opponent down and get on top. Takedowns earn points.

WRESTLING GEAR

MOUTHGUARD
protects the teeth
SINGLET
snug but not too tight

CHAPTER 3

On the

A wrestling bout has two to three periods. Each last two or three minutes. Wrestlers start a period in one of two positions. In one, they are both standing. In the other, they are on their hands and knees. Once wrestlers are in place, the period can begin.

Abraham Lincoln was known for his wrestling skills.

Winning a Bout

Wrestlers win bouts in three ways. One, a wrestler pins both of an opponent's shoulders to the mat. This is called a fall. Two, a wrestler is ahead by many points. In freestyle, it's ten points. In Greco-Roman, it's eight points. This is called a technical fall. And three, the wrestler with the most points at the end of the bout wins.

Pro Wrestling

Freestyle and Greco-Roman wrestling bouts are **amateur**. **Professional** bouts are different. World Wrestling Entertainment (WWE) holds pro fights. It is the biggest pro wrestling company. All Elite Wrestling (AEW) is the second biggest. In both, the wrestlers are athletes. They are also actors. Their bouts follow a **script**. The winner of the fight is often chosen ahead of time.

AMATEURS VS. PROS

AMATEURS	PROS
sports competition	entertainment
no hitting	hitting allowed
follow rules	follow a script
no weapons	weapons allowed
bouts held on a mat	bouts held in a ring

By the Numbers

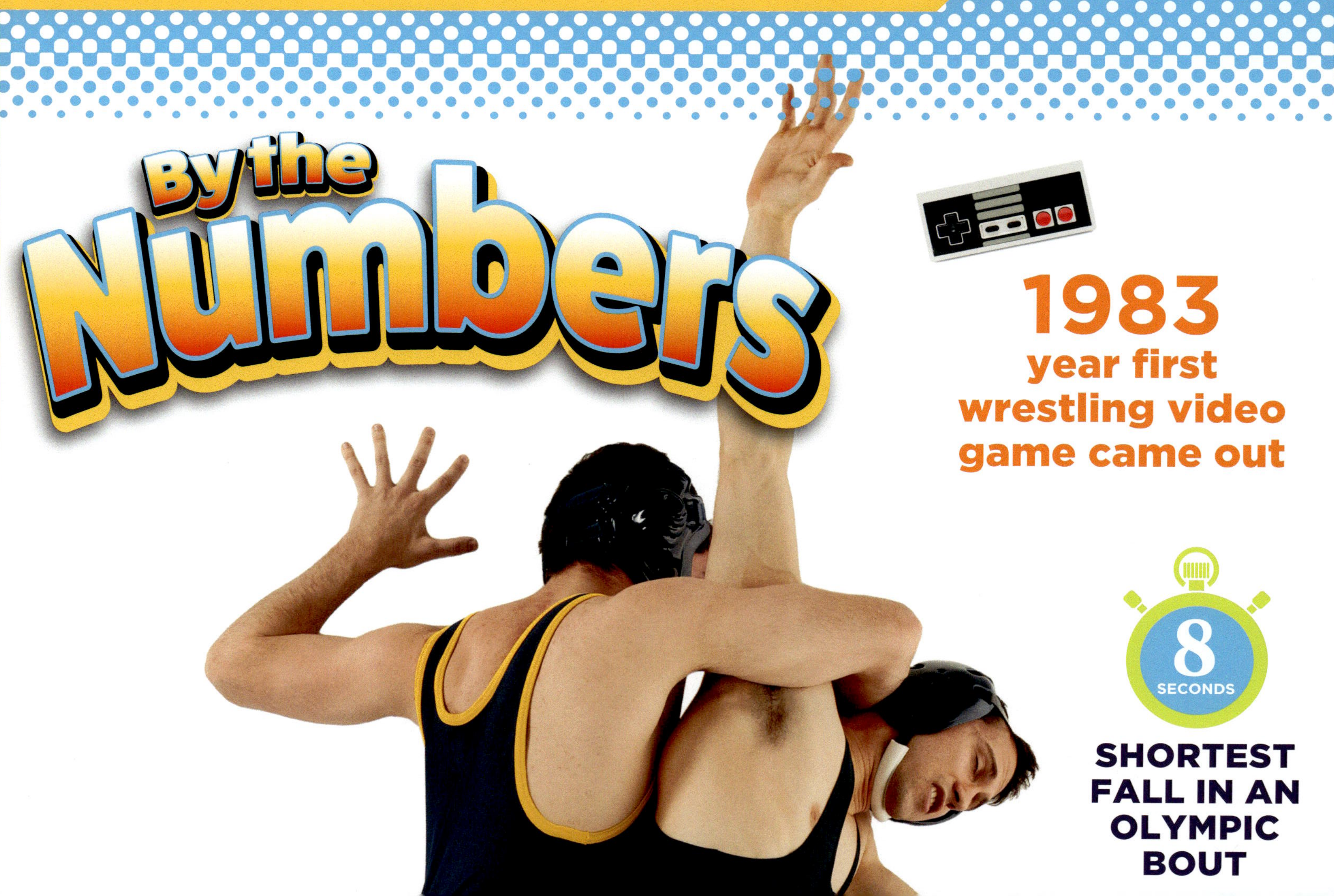

1983
year first wrestling video game came out

8 SECONDS
SHORTEST FALL IN AN OLYMPIC BOUT

21
HOURS
and 44 minutes
LONGEST PRO WRESTLING BOUT, FOUGHT IN JAPAN
2004
YEAR WOMEN'S FREESTYLE WRESTLING JOINED THE OLYMPICS

CHAPTER 4

World Competitions

United World Wrestling (UWW) holds amateur competitions worldwide. They are held throughout the year. Olympic wrestling is also amateur. It occurs every four years. People watch WWE on TV. The fights are watched in 180 countries.

Weight Classes

Wrestlers fight with others in the same weight class. This helps make bouts fair. Each weight class has a top range. Any wrestler under that weight may compete. Often, wrestlers try to get as close to the top weight as possible. It gives them a size advantage during fights.

OLYMPIC WEIGHT CLASSES

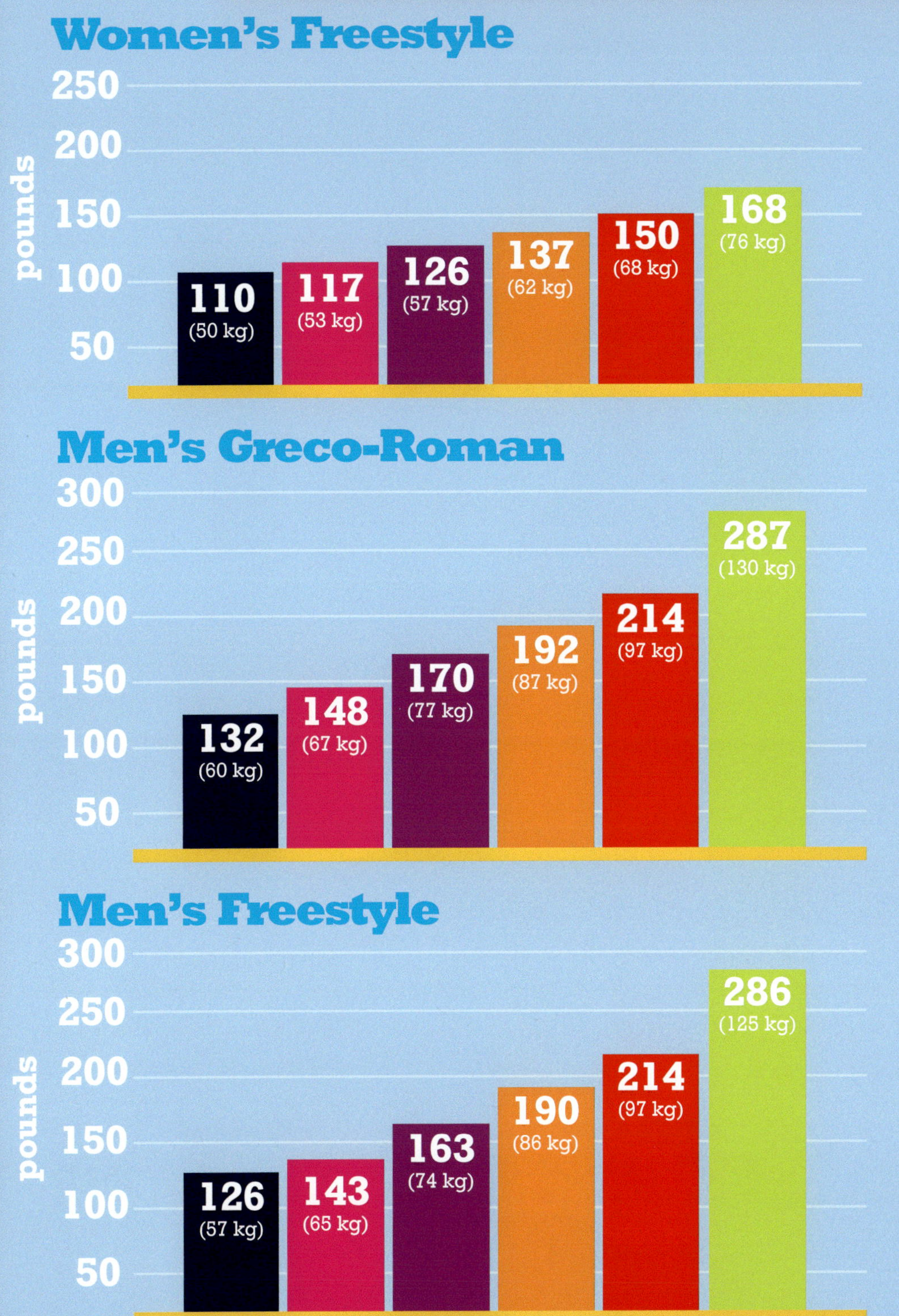

TOP YOUNG WRESTLERS

Amit Elor

is an American wrestler. She won her first UWW gold medal in 2021, at age 17. By 2023, she'd won gold eight more times.

Yui Susaki

is from Japan. She started wrestling at age 13. Since 2010, she has lost only three bouts. Some call her the greatest female wrestler of all time.

Fardin Hedayati

is from Iran. He won his first UWW gold medal in 2022. He was 18 years old. By 2024, he'd won three more.

Gabriel Alejandro Rosillo Kindelan

is from Cuba. He won his first UWW gold medal at age 19. This was followed by eight more golds.

GLOSSARY

amateur (AM-uh-chur)—not paid by an organization to perform

automatic (aw-toh-MAT-ik)—happening or done without thought or effort

bout (BOUT)—a wrestling or boxing contest

endurance (en-DOOR-uhns)—the ability to put up with strain, suffering, or hardship

opponent (uh-POH-nunt)—a person, team, or group that is competing against another

professional (pro-FESH-uh-nuhl)—paid to compete in a sport or activity

script (SKRIPT)—the written form of a play, movie, or TV show

takedown (TAYK-down)—a move that brings someone down to the ground

BOOKS

Anderson, Josh. *Roman Reigns vs. Hulk Hogan: Who Would Win?* Minneapolis: Lerner Publications, 2024.

Arnéz, Lynda. *Be a Pro Wrestler.* Buffalo, NY: Gareth Stevens Publishing, 2024.

Bolte, Mari. *Wrestling.* Mankato, MN: Creative Education and Creative Paperbacks, 2024.

WEBSITES

History of WWE Facts for Kids
kids.kiddle.co/History_of_WWE

Wrestling
kids.britannica.com/kids/article/wrestling/353938

Wrestling
www.cbc.ca/cbckids/olympics/tokyo2020/sports/land/wrestling

INDEX